J
940.54
TON

Tong, Neil

Battles of World War II

Documenting World War II

Battles of
World War II

Neil Tonge

rosen publishing's
**rosen
central**

New York

Published in 2009 by The Rosen Publishing Group Inc.
29 East 21st Street, New York, NY 10010

First Edition

Editor: Camilla Lloyd
Consultants: Dr. R. Gerald Hughes and Dr. James Vaughan
Designer: Phipps Design
Maps: Ian Thompson
Picture researcher: Kathy Lockley
Indexer and proofreader: Patience Coster

Dedicated to Charlie Chandler, a veteran of World War II

Picture Acknowledgments: The author and publisher would like to thank the
following for allowing their pictures to be reproduced in this publication:
Cover photographs: BL: Mary Evans Picture Library, BR: AKG-Images; AKG-Images:
6, 39, 41, 43; © 2006 Alinari/Topfoto.co.uk: 8; Bettman/Corbis: 12, 22, 25, 44;
British Library (12332.c.15)/Heritage-Images: 35; Charlie Chandler: 1, 7, 21, 30;
Corbis: 10; Mary Evans Picture Library: 36; Getty Images (Hulton Archive): 34;
David Pollack/Corbis: 17; RIA Nowosti/AKG-Images: 29; Time & Life Pictures, photo
by Eliot Elisoton/Getty Images: 31, Topfoto.co.uk: 26; Ullstein Bild/AKG-Images: 33.

Library of Congress Cataloging-in-Publication Data

Tong, Neil
  Battles of World War II / Neil Tong. – 1st ed.
      p. cm. -- (Documenting World War II)
  Includes bibliographical references and index.
  ISBN 978-1-4042-1861-1 (lib. bndg.)
  1. Battles of World War 2 2. Battles of World War Two I. Title.
  D743 .T58 2008
  940.54–2 22
                              2007042496

Manufactured in China

CONTENTS

The changing face of war

At the end of World War I (WWI, 1914–1918) it was confidently predicted by many politicians that it had been the war to end all wars. So dreadful had been the conflict and widespread the suffering, it was believed that no country would be so foolish as to declare war ever again. Yet within 20 years of the Treaty of Versailles, which ended WWI, the world was plunged into a more deadly conflict, in September 1939, when Britain and France declared war on Germany, an action that marked the beginning of World War II (WWII).

More soldiers and civilians were to die in WWII than in any war before it. Unlike WWI, which was fought in Europe, few parts of the world would be unaffected by the fighting in WWII.

War on such a vast scale brought into being new ways of fighting and new weapons that changed the course of history forever. Speed and devastation became the hallmarks of the lightning wars, known as *blitzkrieg* (*blitz* is the German word for "lightning") fought by Nazi Germany and Japan in the Pacific. Rapid movements of tanks in close formation, supported by air power, replaced the stalemate of trench warfare, which had characterized WWI. During WWI, the front line barely shifted, since both sides were in trenches and there were few weapons powerful enough to break through each other's defenses. In WWII, bomber aircraft could reach into the heart of enemy territory and strike terror in towns and cities. German forces became the most efficient at fighting such battles, demonstrating their mastery in Poland, Norway, France, the Balkans, and the Soviet Union. Civilians were now on the front line; they were essential to the mass production of weapons that the war depended upon, and as a result, they were also the targets of enemy attack.

New equipment and weapons had evolved toward the end of WWII. They included the jet engine, more effective radar to detect the approach of enemy aircraft, swift-moving, powerful tanks and missiles. Most terrifying of all, the first atomic bombs were dropped in 1945, killing tens of thousands at a stroke in the Japanese cities of Hiroshima and Nagasaki.

The battles of WWII fall broadly into two periods. From 1939–41, the Axis powers (Nazi Germany and fascist Italy in Europe, and Japan in the Far East) won spectacular victories across Europe. France fell to the Nazis in 1940, and Britain stood alone against Germany and Italy, just managing to

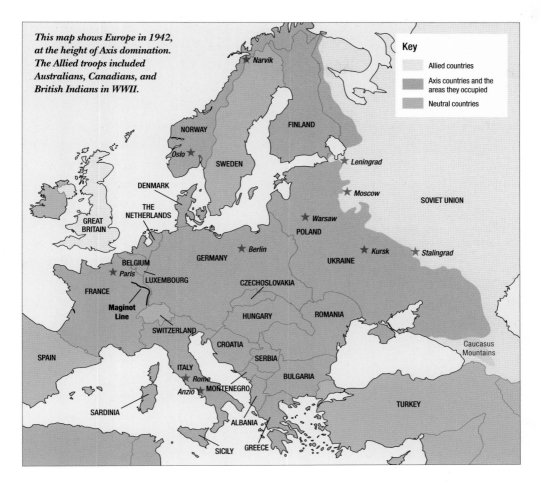

This map shows Europe in 1942, at the height of Axis domination. The Allied troops included Australians, Canadians, and British Indians in WWII.

Key

Allied countries

Axis countries and the areas they occupied

Neutral countries

survive by defeating the German *Luftwaffe* (air force) in the Battle of Britain. In the Far East, Japan, through a series of surprise attacks in 1941–2, overwhelmed many European colonies in Asia.

In the second period from 1941–5, however, the tide of war slowly turned against Germany in favor of the Allies (Britain, the United States, and the Soviet Union, among others), and after 1942, against the Japanese. After being invaded by Germany, the Soviet Union joined the Allied side in 1941. Initially,

Josef Stalin, the communist dictator of the Soviet Union, had signed a nonaggression pact with Germany in 1940 when they jointly invaded Poland.

The U.S.'s entry into the conflict in December 1941 on the side of the Allies was the turning point in the war. It followed the Japanese surprise attack on the U.S. naval base at Pearl Harbor and Japan's rapid expansion in Asia. No other country could match the U.S.'s vast reserves of men and natural resources, and these were to contribute decisively to the Allied victory in WWII.

The military balance: Germany

Adolf Hitler was the Nazi dictator of Germany. He came to power in 1933. Although he had popular support for his early victories in Austria in 1938 and Czechoslovakia in 1939, the majority of the German people

*When Hitler came to power, Germany was militarily and economically weak with high unemployment. One of his solutions was to build **autobahns** (highways). This photo shows Hitler opening the building works at Walserberg in Austria for the construction of an **autobahn** in April 1935.*

dreaded the thought of another major war. German military commanders were not anxious to embark on a total war, because they felt the army was not yet equipped or ready. Yet, when war came, the Germans on the offensive proved to be better prepared than any other European country. The population had been encouraged to prepare for war by the aggressive nationalistic ideology of Nazi propaganda. This promoted the idea that countries were set against one another and only the strongest would survive. Young people, in particular, had been made to believe in this idea at school, through newspapers and movies, and by youth organizations like the Hitler Youth.

The Versailles Treaty, which Germany had been forced to sign in 1919 by the victorious WWI Allies (the U.S., Britain, and France), had limited Germany's army to 100,000 men. Tanks, heavy artillery, aircraft, and submarines were expressly forbidden. From the outset, however, the German government attempted to sidestep these limitations. German forces were secretly trained in other countries during the 1920s, a fact that gradually became known to Britain and France in the 1930s.

After Hitler came to power in 1933, all pretence at obeying the treaty was thrown aside. In October 1933, he announced the expansion of the army to 350,000, and in March 1935, ordered conscription of the male population, setting the strength of the army at 600,000. By 1939, it had reached 730,000 with 1,100,000 men in reserve.

The production of arms and equipment had also been stepped up. Heinz Guderian, a young infantry (ground troops) captain appointed in 1922, became the leading supporter of armored warfare (use of vehicles protected with metal plating).

These Nazi Stuka dive-bomber planes used for blitzkrieg caused havoc in WWII. This picture was taken in Crete in 1941.

By 1931, Guderian had become chief of staff of motorized troops and was pressing for the creation of armored divisions. He met some opposition from those who believed that it was the infantry, marching into battle, who won wars. However, when Hitler came to power, he became an enthusiastic supporter of Guderian's ideas. "*That's what I need,*" he exclaimed when he first saw Guderian's armored unit, "*that's what I want to have!*" By 1939, the armored divisions had grown into the *Panzer* (tank) divisions, which were to strike hard and penetrate deep into enemy territory.

Limited to warships of less than 10,000 tons by the Treaty of Versailles, Germany had built three small "pocket" battleships. These were small battleships that carried heavy firepower. By September 1939, two new 30,000-ton, fast battle cruisers had been built to complement a fleet of five light cruisers, 17 destroyers, and 56 submarines.

Overall, it was the air power Germany had assembled that made it formidable, rather than the *Panzer* armored divisions and new ships. By 1939, Hermann Goering, head of the *Luftwaffe*, had assembled between 4,000 and 4,700 aircraft. These were designed primarily to support the army in striking hard and deep at airfields and concentrations of troops, rather than for "blanket" bombing of cities.

The military balance: Britain and France

Although the French had defeated Germany in 1918 at the end of WWI, they were haunted by the huge loss of life. Out of a French population of fewer than 40 million, 1,385,000 had been killed, and France was now faced with a German population of 68 million. Although the French had a massive army, their equipment had been reduced because of the financial cuts needed to help their economy.

The French defensive system was a long chain of fortifications along the eastern frontier built between the two world wars. This picture shows French soldiers in a railroad tunnel near the Maginot Line. The line proved practically useless in Germany's fast-moving attack in 1940.

Fearing additional future losses of men in battle, the French army changed their tactic of attack to one of defense. André Maginot, minister of defense, fought for the establishment of a huge fortification along the border with Germany, which bore his name and was called the Maginot Line (see the map on page 5). Unfortunately for the French, it did not extend along the border with Belgium, despite the fact that German attack there was seen as a more likely possibility.

The Maginot Line absorbed most of the French defense budget, and as a

result, there was little left to spend on developing an effective type of tank. The generals argued that with the building of an impenetrable defensive line, there would be even less need to fight a highly mobile war.

The French navy, however, was strong and consisted of five battleships, 17 cruisers, 60 destroyers, 70 submarines, two battle cruisers, and two aircraft carriers. This was a powerful fighting force.

France's air force had been largely neglected. The front line defense consisted of 600 fighters, 170 bombers, and 360 reconnaissance aircraft (aircraft that gathered information about the enemy and the fighting conditions). They had no system to warn of attack, and France remained very weak in the air.

Britain was traditionally a world naval power and the navy continued to absorb much of the defense budget. Instead of the vast, conscripted armies of her European neighbors, Britain relied on a small professional volunteer army and troops from the British empire. As a result, Britain only had ten infantry divisions, with 50 cavalry light tanks, and 500 aircraft from the Royal Air Force (RAF) compared with France's 67 divisions.

Britain had led the way in the use of tanks during WWI, but this initiative had faltered. Two British military thinkers, Basil Liddell Hart and John Frederick Charles Fuller, developed the idea of using armored vehicles in concentrated numbers instead of dispersed across the battlefield, but they were largely ignored in Britain. However, their writings were avidly read by German and Soviet commanders, who attempted to put the

SOURCE

LETTER

"We need tanks, of course … but you cannot hope to achieve a real breakthrough with tanks. … As to the air, it will not play the part you expect … It'll be a flash in the pan."

Maurice Gamelin wrote a letter about France's military needs to Paul Reynard, the French premier.

Maurice Gamelin, chief of general staff, to Paul Reynard in the 1930s.

ideas into practice. As the threat of war in the late 1930s loomed large, Britain rushed to produce more aircraft. By September 1939, front line strength had reached 2,075 aircraft; these included the superior *Spitfire* and *Hurricane* fighter aircraft. The bomber force, however, could still easily be shot down by German fighters.

By now, Hitler was turning his attention to the invasion of Poland, as the first step in creating "living space" (or *lebensraum*) for the German people.

The destruction of Poland

The Polish campaign began on September 1, 1939, and offered the ideal opportunity for the Germans to practice *blitzkrieg*. The flat plains of the Polish countryside were easy to invade for a highly mobile force. The campaign was well-timed. The deep, sandy soil of Poland was baked hard after the summer, and this meant that German armor would not get bogged down in the fall rain or winter snow. To prevent the Soviet Union coming to the aid of Poland, Hitler had already struck a deal with its leader, Josef Stalin. Under a secret agreement, known as the Nazi-Soviet Pact, Germany and the Soviet Union agreed to divide Poland in two, with each power taking control of half. Britain and France would only be able to come to the aid of Poland through a strong attack in the west of Europe, but neither country was well enough prepared for war to embark in fighting here at this stage in the conflict.

The Polish army could have fought a better campaign if they had grouped farther back from the frontier, but they did not want to abandon the important industrial areas that were situated on their borders. Furthermore, to have seemed to retreat before the invasion would have hurt Polish national pride.

Worse still, they had grouped most of their army in the "corridor" between East Prussia and Germany, from which they could be attacked on both sides.

The Polish army was quickly overrun by Nazi armored fighting units. German ground forces were supported by attacks by the *Luftwaffe*, who quickly

CARTOON

This political cartoon by a U.S. artist shows Hitler and Stalin as a married couple, allied in the Nazi-Soviet Pact. The caption reads: *"How long will the marriage last?"*

Clifford Kennedy Berryman in June 1941.

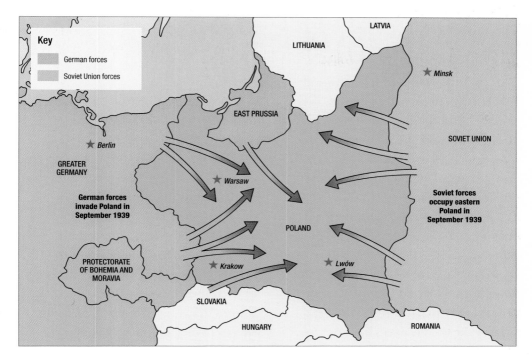

Key

German forces

Soviet Union forces

LATVIA

LITHUANIA

Minsk

EAST PRUSSIA

SOVIET UNION

Berlin

GREATER
GERMANY

Warsaw

**German forces
invade Poland in
September 1939**

**Soviet forces
occupy eastern
Poland in
September 1939**

POLAND

PROTECTORATE
OF BOHEMIA AND
MORAVIA

Krakow

Lwów

SLOVAKIA

HUNGARY

ROMANIA

*This map shows the **blitzkrieg** invasion of Poland in September 1939 by Germany and the Soviet Union.*

knocked out the Polish railroad system and the Polish air force was destroyed. In a matter of days, the rapid advance of the German forces had enveloped the Polish army. With its fighting units cut off, the Polish army ceased to exist except in isolated fragments. By September 8, 1939, German forces had reached Warsaw, having covered 140 miles (225 km) in one week.

On September 10, the Polish commander, Marshal Rydz-Smigly, ordered a general retreat to southeast Poland in the hope of organizing a defensive position. By now, the Germans were beginning to run short of fuel and were desperately tired after their prolonged attacks. The Polish commander, however, was so badly shocked that he was unable to take advantage of the situation. At ground level, Polish cavalry units made heroic but foolhardy attacks on German tanks, and were annihilated.

On September 17, realizing that the German advance was succeeding, the Soviets invaded from the east. The Polish commander in chief fled across the border into Romania.

Only the garrison in Warsaw held out for ten days until it was forced to surrender on October 5,when the last remnants of a few thousand Polish army soldiers surrendered. Meanwhile, Britain and France were slow to respond, and by the time they were fully prepared, Poland was on the point of collapse.

The invasion of Norway

The attention of Nazi Germany and the Allies then turned toward Norway and Denmark (see map on page 5). Both countries were neutral, but the Germans were afraid that Britain might use Norway as a base for Allied troops. The commander in chief of the German Navy, Grand Admiral Erich Raeder, had persuaded Hitler that Norway could provide Germany with secure naval bases and airfields from which Britain could be attacked. Occupation of Norway would also ensure the supply of high grade iron ore to Germany from neighboring Sweden for its armament production.

Denmark was the first country to fall to the Germans. It was invaded by the Nazis on April 9, 1940. Such a small country had no hope of putting up effective resistance and it surrendered to avoid suffering a huge number of casualties.

Hitler had, at first, ignored the requests from his commanders to invade Norway, but when Britain began to lay mines in Norwegian waters, he started to change his mind. By using this as an excuse, namely, by pretending that Germany was anxious

This picture shows German parachute fighters after their descent into southern Norway in 1940.

to prevent an invasion of Denmark and Norway by British and French forces, Hitler made his own aggressive plans.

In Oslo, the capital of Norway, the government tried desperately to stay neutral. However, when the British rescued some of their captured troops from a German ship that had been allowed to shelter in a Norwegian fjord (a deep, water-filled valley connected to the sea), Hitler found the excuse he needed. Hitler argued that the British, not the Germans, had violated Norway's neutrality. On April 3, 1940, German ships carrying troops entered the main Norwegian ports, such as Narvik.

On April 14, German forces struck out from their captured Norwegian bases to the south and west of the country. The Allies attempted to retaliate by landing in the northerly port of Narvik to begin a counterattack. But the strategy failed and the German forces began to link up. The last British force in Narvik finally withdrew when disastrous news of events in France, which was falling to the German army, made their situation in northern Norway difficult to maintain. Deserted by the Allies, the Norwegians had no alternative but to surrender.

The Norwegian campaign fought by Britain was muddled up and poorly carried out. Yet Hitler had almost lost his nerve during the campaign. If Britain and France had pressed home their attacks, they might have achieved more success. However, it is likely that the invasion of France by the Germans in May 1940 would have made it impossible for Britain and France to have kept their toehold in Norway.

After the Polish surrender there followed a curious period, throughout the fall and winter of 1939, when the

SOURCE

SPEECH

"For many generations, Norway ... a tiny army and a population with no desires except to live peaceably ... now fell victims to the new German aggression."

Winston Churchill, prime minister of Britain, in a speech to the House of Commons, London, 1940.

Allies and Germany were at war but when practically no fighting took place. The Germans called it the *sitzkrieg* (the sitting war), the British the "phoney war." The Allies were at a loss about how to proceed. Poland had fallen so rapidly and the Allies had made no plans to launch an offensive attack on Germany in the west. Hitler, meanwhile, was content to let his generals plan the invasion of France, and Britain and France attempted an economic blockade of Germany. In May 1940, this was all to change.

The fall of France

Although the positions of Britain and France appeared to be strong in 1939, in reality they were not. Their combined armies were larger and their navies considerably bigger than those of the Germans, but they were weak in air power and lacked fighting tactics. Together, they could only put 2,700 aircraft into battle while the Germans commanded 4,000 aircraft; and although they had as many tanks as the Germans, they had scattered them among the infantry units and had only a few armored divisions. Above all, the Germans had perfected a new type of warfare, as they had demonstrated in their campaigns in Poland and Norway. German air power, armored units, and infantry blended together to form powerful punching attacks that were almost irresistible.

On May 10, 1940, the German attack in the west began. Paratroopers were dropped from aircraft in the skies over the Netherlands and Belgium, countries that had tried to stay neutral. They were soon joined by swift-moving German armored divisions and infantry, which streamed across the border. British and French forces slowly moved in to meet them. But this was only a ruse on the part of the Germans, for their main attack was to come farther east in the Ardennes (a region of extensive forests in Belgium

and Luxembourg that stretched into France). This was a hilly area of France that was considered unsuitable for tank attack. The Maginot Line, in which the French had put so much trust, was merely bypassed (see map on page 5).

SOURCE

RADIO SPEECH

"What General Weygand [the French commander] called the Battle of France is over. I expect that the Battle of Britain is about to begin. The whole fury and might of the enemy must be very soon turned on us. Let us, therefore, be prepared to do our duty so that, if the British Empire lasts for a thousand years, men will say, 'This was their finest hour'."

Radio broadcast by Winston Churchill, 1940.

Guderian, the German tank commander, successfully broke through the French lines at Sedan and hurtled toward the ports on the English Channel. On May 20, just ten days after the invasion, he reached the coast. The Battle for France was all but won (see map on opposite page). The main units of the British and French forces were driven into increasingly smaller groups, hemmed in by the Channel coast. Half a million Allied soldiers were now trapped around the port of Dunkirk, and total destruction seemed imminent. But then, on May 24, the German advance suddenly halted at Hitler's orders. No one is quite sure why this happened. It may have been to refuel the German tanks and provide rest for the soldiers before they began the final assault on what appeared to be a defeated enemy.

This pause in the proceedings gave the British time to set up a rescue operation. A fleet of small boats launched from the southeast coast of Britain managed to evacuate 340,000 mainly British troops before Dunkirk was finally taken by the Germans on June 4.

On May 15, 1940, the Netherlands had surrendered, Belgium had followed on May 28, and an undefended Paris was occupied on June 14. The French government had fled south, after briefly considering continuing the fight from France's North African colonies. This idea was abandoned, and it was left to the ageing Marshal Pétain, hero of WWI, to seek a peace treaty with Germany. Finally, on June 22, France signed the surrender terms with Germany in the same railroad car that had been used by the French to accept Germany's surrender in 1918. Northern and eastern France were occupied by the

Germans, but the remainder was given to the French under Marshal Pétain, known as "Vichy" France after the town of Vichy. The Vichy government was expected to carry out German instructions.

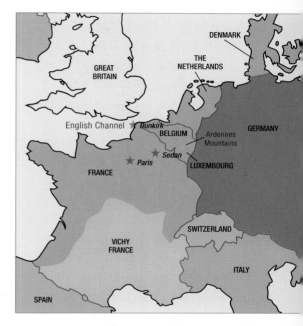

This map shows the areas involved in the fall of France to Nazi Germany in 1940.

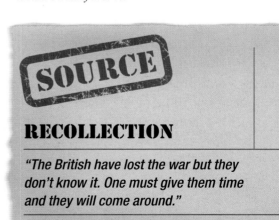

SOURCE

RECOLLECTION

"The British have lost the war but they don't know it. One must give them time and they will come around."

Adolf Hitler in a conversation with party members in June 1940, later recalled by other Nazi leaders.

The Battle of Britain

Hitler expected Britain to ask for peace terms, but instead the British were defiant. Although most of the British army had been successfully evacuated from Dunkirk, they had lost all their equipment. The air force was small compared to the *Luftwaffe*, and the navy was unable to repel the attacks by German submarines on its convoys (groups of ships protected by warships).

The German commanders in charge of coordinating attacks had prepared a plan for the invasion of Britain called Operation Sea Lion. A quarter of a million German troops were to be transported across the Channel, but for the plan to succeed, it was vital that the Germans secured supremacy in the air. Hitler therefore ordered the *Luftwaffe* to destroy the RAF. Despite being outnumbered in terms of its aircraft, Britain possessed two very good fighter planes, the *Spitfire* and the *Hurricane*. The German *Messerschmitt* came in a close second to these, but the other German fighters could not achieve the technical capabilities of the British aircraft. Most importantly, the RAF possessed radar, a system that detected approaching aircraft.

The Battle of Britain began on August 8, 1940. By August 23, most of the RAF airfields had been destroyed but then, unexpectedly, British fortunes changed. A few German aircraft bombers had accidentally bombed the city of London and killed civilians. In retaliation, the British prime minister, Winston Churchill, ordered a bomber raid on Berlin. Hitler flew into a rage and ordered the *Luftwaffe* to bomb British cities in revenge, especially the capital, London, instead of the airfields.

SOURCE

SPEECH

"Wars are not won by evacuation [Dunkirk]. Even though large tracts of Europe and many old and famous states have fallen or may fall into the grip of the Gestapo [German secret police] ... we shall not flag or fail. We shall fight in France, we shall fight in the seas and the oceans ... we shall fight on the beaches, we shall fight on the landing grounds, we shall fight in the fields and the streets ... we shall never surrender."

Winston Churchill in a House of Commons speech on June 4, 1940.

Each night, from September 7 to mid-May 1941, German aircraft dropped bombs on British cities. This

"NEVER WAS SO MUCH OWED BY SO MANY TO SO FEW" *THE PRIME MINISTER*

POSTER

This British poster includes the famous line from a speech made by Churchill on August 20, 1940. The poster advertises a film about the war, released in 1942.

phase of the war became known as the Blitz, after the German word *blitzkrieg*. More than 10,000 people were killed in London alone, and over 1.5 million houses were destroyed or damaged. London was not the only place to suffer. From October 1941 onward, other British cities were bombed. One of the most devasting raids took place in Coventry on December 14, when more than 600 tons of bombs were dropped over the city. More than 500 people died. The bombing of the cities preoccupied the *Luftwaffe* giving the British an opportunity to repair their airfields and destroy the German invasion fleet on the other side of the Channel. On September 15, the RAF repelled two massive German air attacks on London, and Hitler had to abandon the operation.

Although Britain stood little chance of breaking the Nazi hold on Europe alone, it provided a base for operations against the Axis powers. There was a Polish government in exile, and a government of the Free French under the exiled De Gaulle in London.

The Battle of the Atlantic

Keeping Britain supplied with food and equipment was vital to its survival. The Germans aimed to starve Britain into submission by attacking the convoy routes of shipping through the Mediterranean and from West Africa, but most importantly, from across the Atlantic. Although the United States did not officially enter the war until December 1941, it was the main source of Britain's supplies in the early years of WWII.

At the start of the war, German submarines (known as U-boats) were sinking British ships in increasing numbers. The British tried to protect themselves by sailing in convoys. The antisubmarine force available to Britain was small, just 150 destroyers, which meant that only two destroyers could be assigned to each convoy. Fortunately, the Germans had only 48 operational submarines at the beginning of the war, so the attacks on British convoys for the first eight months were fairly limited. The ships in the convoys protected themselves with a type of radar, called "asdic." When a submarine was detected, the British ships would fire depth charges (explosives that detonated under the water) that could sink or damage the submarines. The British also relied on the Enigma machine that could code

STATISTICS

This graph shows total British merchant shipping losses from September 1939 to December 1941 (thousand gross tons).

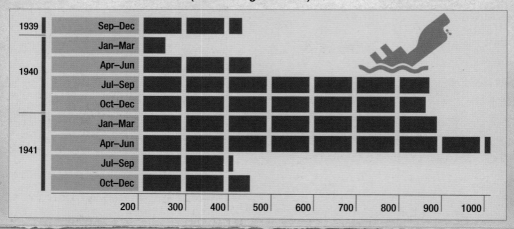

and decode secret messages. Their ability to decrypt the German military communications helped the Allies enormously. This intelligence was codenamed *ULTRA*.

The fall of France gave Germany additional naval bases from which they could attack the British convoys. To avoid being detected by the asdic, the U-boats concentrated on lone ships or ones that had "straggled" from the main convoy. The most vulnerable area of attack was in the mid-Atlantic, about 200 miles west of Ireland. This was the point at which destroyers had to leave the convoys to take up escort duty of the homeward-bound ships.

The U-boats kept in contact through their radios so that they could attack in "wolf packs," stringing themselves out across the line of the convoy. To achieve this, they had to be on the surface during the day to maintain contact, and sometimes they attacked the convoys from the surface at night. Submerging was the only way for the submarines to escape, and the faster escort ships could then drop depth charges to sink them. The best form of defense against the U-boats was the long-range bomber, but there were few of them and they were being used for various other missions. Gradually, as the production of these planes rose, they were released for escort duty (protection of the supply ships). At one point, Britain's shipping losses exceeded replacements by 7,000,000

SOURCE

RECOLLECTION

"The American captain was in a lifeboat with a steward who was in a very bad way, mainly from exposure and swallowing oil. The boat was on the weatherside [toward the wind] of the ship, and one moment level with the rail, the next 30 feet below us. We managed to grab the captain eventually when the boat was on the upsurge, but couldn't get the steward. We steamed in a circle, not easy in the weather we were having, and got the boat on our lee side [side sheltered from the wind].
We got the man in, but he died shortly afterward."

A U.S. sublieutenant describes how his escort ship helped to rescue survivors from a convoy in 1943.

tons. But with increased numbers of escort ships, in late 1941–2, Britain was able to gradually recover the losses.

On December 7, 1941, the situation changed with Japan's attack on Pearl Harbor. Hitler declared war on the U.S., and suddenly the neutral security zone protecting merchant shipping, along the eastern seaboard of the U.S., was gone. Despite the end to neutrality, the Allies were gradually able to gain the upper hand by 1943 as their superior forces overwhelmed the Germans.

Blitzkrieg in the Balkans and North Africa

On October 15, 1940, Benito Mussolini, the dictator of Italy and Germany's ally, hurriedly began preparations for an attack on Greece from Italian bases in southern Albania. Hitler hoped that Mussolini would not go through with the attack since he felt Italy was unprepared. However, on October 28, Mussolini jubilantly announced to Hitler when they met at the railroad station in Florence, Italy, that his troops had already crossed the Greek border. The Italian expedition was disastrous from the start. A whole division was wiped out. Within 11 days, the Greeks had taken 5,000 Italians prisoner. Rain and snow worsened the treacherous conditions over mountain passes and gorges. The Italians were pushed back and the Greek army advanced 30 miles within Albania's borders, inflicting 30,000 casualties.

It was clear to Hitler that, as Germany's allies, the Italians would have to be rescued. Diplomatic agreements had been reached with Romania, Bulgaria, and Hungary that German troops would be stationed there prior to the invasion of the entire Balkan region. Yugoslav resistance lasted only 12 days. Then Italian, Hungarian, and Bulgarian forces, which were allied with Germany, moved toward Greece for the kill.

Key

Areas governed by Vichy France

Areas under Axis occupation

Areas under Allied power

Neutral states

Nazi-occupied France

Movements of Axis troops (red) and Allied troops (green)

This map shows the farthest advance of the Axis powers across the Balkans and North Africa in 1942.

Meanwhile, a British force landed in Macedonia, to the east of Albania, to assist the Greeks. But the might of the German army was too great, and the British and Greek forces were forced back. Fifty-thousand British troops managed to escape to the safety of Egypt, but thousands of their troops were taken captive. Once again, Germany's *blitzkrieg* tactics had won the day in the Balkans.

The war had also spread to the European colonies of North Africa. In September 1940, Italian Field Marshal Rodolfo Graziani launched an attack from Italy's colony in Libya against the British in Egypt. Although the Italian troops were vastly superior in numbers, they were repulsed, and streams of prisoners were taken into British captivity. The British then pushed rapidly across North Africa, virtually ending Italian dominance there. However, the demand for British soldiers to fight the Greek campaign cut short an otherwise successful campaign in Africa.

On February 14, 1942, German General Erwin Rommel arrived in Tunisia with an advance party of troops, which were to become the advance guard of the Afrika Corps (a German unit formed to fight in North Africa). On March 31, the Afrika Corps attacked the British. German speed was

RECOLLECTION

"We woke up one morning and everything was being bombed by German planes. The next day, German Gliders and paratroopers crash landed."

In 2007, Charlie Chandler recalls the *blitzkrieg* in Crete in 1941, shortly before his troop was evacuated to Egypt.

This photo was taken in the Mena Camp in Egypt in 1941. The haste of the evacuation from Crete meant that these British soldiers arrived with only their clothes and a few personal possessions. Members of this troop were captured by the Germans in 1942 and became prisoners of war in the Benghazi Camp, Libya.

again decisive and the British were sent reeling back into Egypt. On June 23, 1942, Rommel crossed the Egyptian border. The British position in the Middle East was now close to collapse.

The bombing of Pearl Harbor

Early in the morning of December 7, 1941, 353 Japanese planes, launched from six aircraft carriers, attacked the U.S. naval base at Pearl Harbor, Hawaii. This was the culmination of a deteriorating relationship between the two countries. The U.S., as a power in the Pacific, was concerned about Japan's expansion through China, and as a result, had imposed limits on the export of war materials to Japan. In May 1940, President Franklin Delano Roosevelt ordered the transfer of the Pacific fleet from San Diego in California to Pearl Harbor in the Hawaiian Islands.

The Japanese response was to make an alliance with Germany and Italy, in which they would come to one another's aid if attacked. This alliance was a hostile gesture toward the U.S.

In January 1941, the U.S. ambassador to Japan heard rumors of a planned attack on Pearl Harbor, but the reports were dismissed as "fantastic" by the U.S. commanders. In fact, the Japanese admiral, Isoroku Yamamoto, really was planning to attack Pearl Harbor, because he believed that knocking out the U.S.'s Pacific fleet in one decisive blow would allow Japan to gain control of the Pacific.

This is a picture of the Japanese pilot, Nobuo Fujita, who took part in the bombing of Pearl Harbor.

The United States attempted to find a diplomatic solution to the looming conflict but its proposals proved unacceptable to the Japanese. Japan pretended to continue with the negotiations in order to mask its preparations for an attack on Pearl Harbor. Japanese insistence that the U.S. respond to their proposals to remove the sanctions on their oil imports by 1:00 p.m. on December 6 alerted the U.S. government to the possibility that an attack might take place after that date. A warning was sent to Pearl Harbor, but through a series of mishaps, the warning was not acted upon.

On the morning of December 7, the Japanese task force arrived 200 miles (322 km) north of Pearl Harbor without being detected. Japan's subsequent attack was devastating to the U.S. fleet. Eighteen ships were hit and more than 200 aircraft destroyed or damaged, and 2,400 Americans were killed. Fortunately for the U.S., all of its aircraft carriers were at sea at the time. Although the Japanese stole the advantage here, the bombing was to lead to their defeat in the long run. Japan's actions brought the U.S. into the war on the side of Britain. The vast resources that the U.S. could bring to bear on the war led to the decisive turning point that resulted in the Allied victory. However, directly after the Pearl Harbor attack, Japan did make a series of rapid gains in 1942.

RECOLLECTION

"I was told [the Japanese would] attempt a surprise attack on Pearl Harbor using all their military facilities. He added that although the project seemed fantastic, the fact that he had heard it from many sources prompted him to pass on the information. My colleague told a member of my staff that he had heard from many sources, including a Japanese source, that the Japanese military forces planned, in the event of a failure of negotiations, to attack Pearl Harbor."

Joseph Grew, the U.S. ambassador in Tokyo, January 27, 1941.

SPEECH

"December 7 is a date which will live in infamy."

President Roosevelt's reaction to the Japanese bombing of Peal Harbor.

President Franklin D. Roosevelt in a speech to the U.S. Congress in December 1941.

War in the Pacific

After the bombing of Pearl Harbor, the Japanese made a series of rapid gains in early 1942. They captured many of the islands dotted across the western Pacific. Allied colonies on mainland Asia also fell to them. The French Vichy government, under German pressure, agreed to a Japanese occupying force in their colonies in Indo-China. From here, the Japanese launched successful attacks on Malaya, Singapore, and Burma, and were soon at the borders of British-controlled India. Japan attempted to defend its new empire and to cut off Australia from the U.S. to the south with a short *blitzkrieg* war before the full industrial might of the U.S. could swing into action against them (see map on page 27).

The naval battle of the Coral Sea, in May 1942, was the opening battle in the Pacific War. Neither the U.S. nor the Japanese fleet saw the others' ships, and all the fighting took place between aircraft flying from aircraft carriers. The Japanese had to withdraw, but not before inflicting considerable damage on the U.S. fleet.

In June, 150 Japanese warships steamed toward the island of Midway. The U.S. had only 76 ships but did have the advantage of knowing the Japanese naval codes and their movements through their intelligence networks. However, the U.S. suffered severe losses inflicted by the Japanese *Zero* fighter (a lightweight fighter aircraft) and Japanese bombers damaged the U.S. airfields on Midway. In retaliation, the U.S. launched its

BOOK

"All through the Pacific and the Far East in 1941, I heard about the worthlessness of those 'little monkeys' [the Japanese]. Everywhere, I heard what we would do to them when the day of the great pushover came. One cruiser and a couple of aircraft would destroy Tokyo."

Ernest Hemingway in *Men at War*, written in 1942.

slow-moving *Devastator* torpedo bombers. Most of these were destroyed, but they distracted the *Zero* fighters long enough for 54 U.S. dive-bombers to pounce. Within minutes, three Japanese aircraft carriers had been hit and chaos spread. Although more fighting would take place around Midway, that day, June 7, 1942, had decided the final outcome of the battle. Without air cover, the Japanese fleet could not survive, so the fleet had

U.S. Marines disembark at Guadalcanal.
The Japanese fought ferociously and often chose
death over the humiliation of capture.

to steam homeward. Japan's eastward expansion was halted.

At Guadalcanal in the south Pacific in 1942, the Japanese began building an airfield to break communications between the U.S. and Australia. U.S. Marines landed in August in their first offensive operation against Japanese-held territory. A long struggle followed since both sides lacked supplies, but the U.S. expelled the Japanese. Guadalcanal was the first of many battles that allowed the U.S. to tighten the net around the Japanese Empire.

The Burma campaign

Burma was attractive to the Japanese for two reasons (see the map opposite). First, if Japan could control Burma completely then it could cut off the Allied overland supplies currently being sent to the Chinese nationalist government forces, who were fighting against Japan. Second, Burma could act as a base for attack against the British colony, India. The British, who were fighting many battles in several theaters of war, could only put together a scratch force (available soldiers that were often less highly trained than most) and were easily pushed back to India's borders.

There followed a number of months when both sides probed the others' defenses, looking for weak points to attack. The stalemate in India between the two sides was only eased by the arrival of Brigadier Orde Wingate, who organized British troops in guerrilla operations, in which they were dropped behind enemy lines in order to disrupt communications.

The British command in Burma was

British and British Indian forces in action in Mandalay in 1945. Mandalay is the second largest city in Burma (Burma is today called Myanmar).

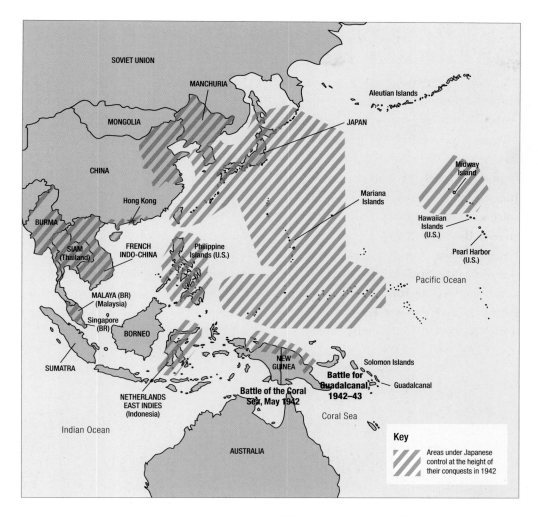

This map shows the extent of Japanese conquests in the Pacific in 1942. The labels "BR" and "U.S." refer to the areas that were controlled by the British and the United States before the bombing of Pearl Harbor.

overhauled in 1943 with the appointment of Field Marshal Slim, commander of the British 14th Army. Hope returned to the Allied forces as the troops became better organized. Between March and July 1944, fierce but inconclusive battles took place in Burma, in which neither side gained any real advantage. Japan decided to launch an out-and-out attack on the strategic towns of Imphal and Kohima on the borders of India. However, the Japanese were gradually forced back by the British and the British Indian troops, who were secure in the support of Allied air power. Early in 1945, victory was in sight for the Allies, and while the Burma campaign did not directly impact the outcome of the war, it did restore morale and confidence to the British troops.

Barbarossa and Stalingrad

Despite constant warnings from the Allies, Stalin was taken completely off guard by the massive attacks by German and Axis forces on the Soviet Union in Operation Barbarossa on June 22, 1941. Whole Soviet armies were surrounded in the lightning strikes. By the end of September, Leningrad was completely cut off from the rest of the Soviet Union, and by October, German forces were 60 miles (97 km) from Moscow. It appeared as if the German *blitzkrieg* tactics had

worked again. Hitler was so confident of victory, he boasted, *"I declare and declare it without reservation that the enemy in the east has been struck down and will never rise again."* But a surprise attack by the Soviets drove the German forces back 150 miles (241 km). The bitterly cold weather and impassable mud forced both sides to sit out the winter.

The following summer, a huge German offensive took place, aimed at capturing the Caucasus' oil fields. The River Volga was reached on August 23,

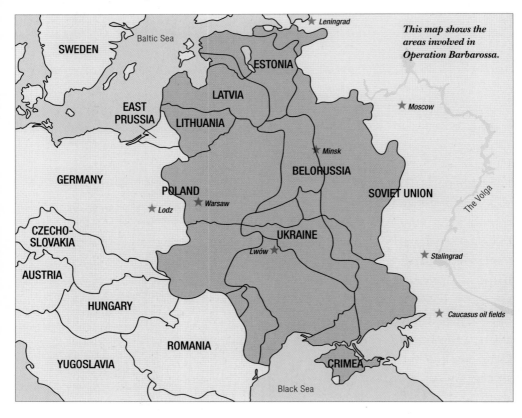

This map shows the areas involved in Operation Barbarossa.

1943 and Stalingrad besieged.

Stalingrad (today called Volgograd) stands on an immense bend as the River Volga sweeps eastward. In 1941, the town was a communications center and as long as it remained in Soviet hands, the German armies that were attacking the oil fields were threatened with an assault on their flank. The German 6th Army, under General Friedrich von Paulus, was ordered to attack and take the city. The Soviets fought the invading Germans over every house and every street. By November 1943, the Germans had reduced the Soviet position to a few hundred yards along the river. Meanwhile, the Soviet commander, Marshal Georgi Zhukov, had been preparing a vast force for a counterattack. After four days, he had closed a pincer movement (attacking an enemy force from two sides) around von Paulus' 6th Army. Hitler ordered von Paulus to keep fighting, but when a German attack to relieve the besieged forces was beaten off by the Soviets, the Nazis were doomed. On January 31, 1943, von Paulus surrendered his army, much to Hitler's anger. Only 91,000 men remained of the 300,000 who had entered the city. In Churchill's words, the Soviets had *"torn the guts out"* of the Germans, and from now on, the vast reserves of Soviet manpower were prepared to drive the enemy back.

The first German field marshal ever to surrender, von Paulus (on the left of the picture) leads the remnants of the 6th Army from Stalingrad into captivity.

RECOLLECTION

"We have fought for over 15 days for a single house with mortars, machine guns and bayonets. Already by the third day, 54 German corpses lay slain in the cellars, on the landings, and the staircases. Stalingrad is no longer a town. By day, it is an enormous cloud of burning, blinding smoke … a vast furnace lit by the reflection of the flames. And when night comes, one of those scorching, howling, bleeding nights, the dogs plunge into the Volga and swim desperately to gain the other bank. The nights of Stalingrad are a terror to them."

A German officer during the Battle for Stalingrad, 1942–3.

The Battle of El Alamein

While the Soviets were holding on to Stalingrad by their fingertips and the U.S. troops were celebrating victory at Midway, the German general, Erwin Rommel, had been giving British forces a pounding in the deserts of North Africa. However, despite his rapid advance his supply position was desperate. The British had managed to hang on to the island of Malta in the eastern Mediterranean (see the map on page 20), despite the fierce battering it had taken. From this island base, they were able to keep the British army supplied in Egypt while disrupting Rommel's supplies.

A new British commander, Bernard Montgomery, was appointed and he

These soldiers from submachine group "B" of the 64th Medium Royal Artillery stand in front of their submachine gun in Egypt, North Africa. The troops were organized into groups (A, B, C, and D) and there were ten men in each group.

began to prepare for a counterattack. British tanks outnumbered the German tanks by two to one (1,029 British to 496 German) and the British also had overall air superiority. Also, although it was not known at the time, Rommel was sick and had been flown back to a hospital in Germany. The Battle of El Alamein lasted from October 23 to November 4, 1942. It followed a lengthy confrontation between the Axis and the Allies over the port of Tobruk in Libya, which took place between March and November 1941. The Allies eventually secured victory in Tobruk.

At El Alamein, Rommel had been flown back to join his Afrika Corps, but he could not find an answer to Montgomery's attacks. As the Afrika Corps reeled back westward, an Anglo-American army was landing behind

These U.S. soldiers survey destroyed German equipment in North Africa in 1943.

them in Morocco and Algeria in Operation Torch (November 1942).

Morocco, Algeria, and Tunisia were controlled by Germany's ally, Vichy France, and there was some doubt as to whether they might defect to the Allies. As it turned out, there was little French resistance and consequently few casualties on the Allied side. By February 24, 1943, the retreating German forces had prepared a formidable defense line in Tunisia. To make matters worse, the Allied command was divided. The French would not obey orders from the British, and cooperation between British and U.S. troops was poor. The Allies decided that command structures needed to be simplified, with one commander in charge. On May 7, Tunis, the capital of Tunisia, was captured by the Allies, and by the end of May, Axis resistance was over. *"We are masters of the North African shore,"* declared Churchill. The Nazis either surrendered or were wiped out by the British Royal Navy as they attempted to escape to mainland Italy and Sicily.

The Italian campaign

Since the fall of 1942, a continual debate had taken place between British and U.S. military planners on where they should next focus their attention in the war against Germany. There were many possibilities, among them Sicily, the Greek mainland, Yugoslavia, or southern France. The Soviets were anxious to see another front opened up by the Allies on mainland Europe, to take the pressure off their fighting forces. In the end, Churchill won the day with his proposal to attack the *"soft underbelly of Europe,"* namely Italy. However, the conquest of the Italian peninsula was to prove, in the words of U.S. Commander General Clarke, *"a tough old gut"* (see map on page 5.).

The successful campaign in Sicily in the summer of 1942 and the fall of the Italian dictator, Mussolini, in September encouraged those who favored an out-and-out campaign in Italy. The Germans reacted quickly, occupying a defensive line, the Gustav Line south of Rome, which proved very difficult to crack. The most formidable part of the defenses was Monte Cassino, a rocky hill some 80 miles (130 km) south of Rome, crowned by a famous sixth-century monastery with massive walls. Until Monte Cassino was taken, it would be impossible to reach Rome. However,

Monte Cassino defied every attempt by the Allies to bomb the Germans into submission. On the eastern side of Italy, Montgomery forced a crossing of the River Sangro against fierce fire power. Rain had turned the mountain

SOURCE

DIARY

"Stop briefly at 1:00 a.m. and sleep where we drop. No sleep last night and evidently very little tonight. One meal only yesterday. At 2:00 a.m. men line the road, fallen by the wayside dead-beat. I can't go much farther. I am nearly done. It is pitch black here in the avenues of woods. I am sweating with weakness. At 2:30 a.m., we overtake men of the Patricias [Italians] and kip down. The sun rises at 8:15 and warms us as we march off. Soon we near the summit of Mount Basilica … Settle at 1:30 p.m. at a big convalescent hospital for children and sleep for six hours in a real bed. Had almost forgotten it was the Sabbath. Have a feeling God will understand…"

British Captain Roy Durnford, regimental chaplain, Seaforth Highlanders, in his diary, September 4, 1943.

British troops operate a 40mm antiaircraft gun during the battles around Monte Cassino, Italy, in the spring of 1944.

roads into raging streams and a bitterly cold winter set in. By Christmas Day, 1943, the Allies had been forced to a grinding halt. They discussed a way to get around the problem. Rather than crawl up the leg of Italy, it was suggested that they should make an amphibious landing on the beaches of Anzio, behind the Gustav Line.

The landings took the Germans by surprise. The first the Germans heard of the plan was the report from a fighter pilot that a full-scale invasion was underway. The Allies then lost the advantage, and instead of striking into the interior and forming a bridgehead (an advanced position in enemy territory), the U.S. commander waited for reinforcements. The Germans took the advantage and counterattacked. So fierce was the fighting that the Allies did not break out from the bridgehead until May 23, almost four months after the first landings.

The Battle of Kursk

After the terrible defeat at Stalingrad, Hitler had handed some control back to the *Wehrmacht* (armed forces) and his General Staff, particularly to Guderian, who had achieved so many spectacular tank victories in the past. The Soviets had become dangerously overstretched, particularly around the town of Kursk about halfway between Moscow and Stalingrad, a "pocket" from which the Germans were in a position to attack on three sides.

The Germans hoped that they might be able to crush the Soviets in the Kursk pocket and force them to retreat. They would then follow this up with a drive to the southeast. A massive tank force was assembled to carry out the attack. Hitler, however, hesitated in giving the order and the plan was not put into action until July 3, 1944. The Soviets were already prepared, because their intelligence officers had warned them in advance of the attack and they were able to put up a fierce resistance.

The fighting around Kursk turned out to be one of the biggest tank battles in history. On July 12, 1944, 850 Soviet tanks fought nearly 750 German tanks. There were almost 200,000

The conflict between the Soviet and German forces in Kursk in 1943 is considered the largest armored battle in history.

Soviet and 50,000 German casualties within the first ten days of fighting.

The German offensive petered out since they could not match the reserves that the Soviet army could throw into the battle, and soon the Germans were pushed back. The Germans simply could not match the Soviet manpower nor meet their production of tanks. Although the Germans could only produce 4,800 tanks in 1942, the Soviets had already produced 24,400, and were also receiving additional supplies from the United States.

The Battle of Kursk proved to be another turning point in the course of the war. The Germans had lost so much equipment, weapons, and men that they could now no longer launch a major offensive in the east. From now on, the Germans would be forced to make a fighting withdrawal.

BOOK

"The battlefield seemed too small for the hundreds of armored machines … The detonation of the guns merged into a continuous howl. … Shells fired at short range penetrated both front and side armor of the tanks. While this was going on, there were frequent tank explosions as ammunition blew up, while tank turrets, blown off by the explosions, were thrown dozens of meters away from the twisted machines."

From the *Official Soviet History* written by Soviet military historians shortly after WWII. It is describing the Battle of Kursk.

CARTOON

This Soviet caricature depicts Hitler as an object held in pincers above a barrel by the gloved hands of the Allies (the U.S., Britain, and the Soviet Union). It was published in Moscow in the Soviet Union in 1943.

From a collection called *Hitler and His Gang* by Boris Efimovich Fridyland, Moscow 1943.

The D-Day landings

Since 1942, Stalin had been pressing the Allies to open up a new front in German-occupied France. The launch of a seaborne invasion on the northern French coast was a huge risk and would need all the organizational skills of the Allies. The south of Britain was turned into one vast military camp. Operation Overlord, the codename given to the

U.S. troops wade through sea and enemy fire in the D-Day landings.

invasion of France, was finally ready in the early summer of 1944. There were nerve-racking days as the Allies waited for decent weather.

On June 6, General Dwight Eisenhower, the Allied commander, gave the order for D-Day (Deliverance Day) to begin. More than a thousand

bombers attacked the coastal defenses of northern France, and thousands of paratroopers were dropped inland under the cover of darkness. The Allies had fooled the Germans into thinking that they were landing elsewhere on the French coast; they also had complete air superiority.

More than a thousand ships headed for the beaches of Normandy, codenamed Utah, Gold, Juno, Sword, and Omaha. By nightfall on D-Day, 156,000 Allied troops were ashore along a bridgehead 30 miles (50 km) long. On some of the beaches they had met little opposition, but there had been severe fighting on Omaha beach where U.S. forces had been pinned down by Axis troops and had suffered heavy casualties.

The D-Day landings had been a success but Normandy proved to be a difficult place in which to fight. Narrow country lanes and high hedges were easy places to hide. Casualties mounted as the battles raged across Normandy.

The British were forced into a stalemate around Caen while U.S. troops seized the port of Cherbourg.

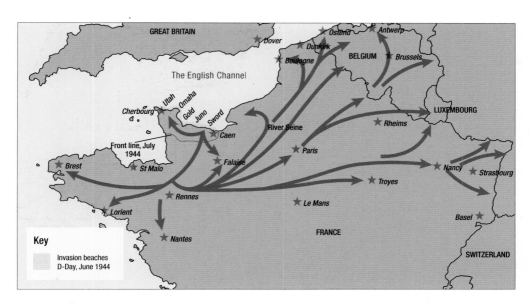

This map shows the Allied invasion of northwest Europe in Operation Overlord in the summer of 1944.

The U.S. general, George S. Patton, then smashed through the German defenses, catching a huge German force in the Falaise Gap. Thousands of Germans were killed and over 50,000 taken prisoner. The way was now open for the Allies to retake Paris. The Nazis lost 450,000 men in Normandy, with 210,000 taken as prisoners. The victory had cost the Allies 206,000 casualties, 37,976 of whom were fatally wounded. As the Allies neared the capital, Paris, the secret resistance groups in France rose and retook the city.

In September 1944, Montgomery suggested that the Allied forces take a shortcut into Germany by seizing a number of bridgeheads across the River Rhine. Eisenhower was doubtful that this could be achieved and preferred to advance on a broad front (advancing steadily at all points). Despite his reluctance, Eisenhower gave Montgomery the go-ahead. The Battle of Arnhem, named after the last Dutch town before the Rhine and Germany, was not a success, with Allied lines stretched so thin that the Germans were easily able to cut them off. Brussels and Antwerp fell, however, but much of the Netherlands remained in German hands as winter began.

In mid-December, Hitler launched his last military surprise, the Battle of the Bulge. Against the advice of his generals, he counterattacked through the Ardennes Mountains. The Germans were at first successful, driving the U.S. back, but lack of fuel soon put an end to the advance. Within a month, they were pushed back and had lost 120,000 men. The troops' hopes of defending Germany were greatly weakened.

The bombing of Germany

During the first years of the war, the Allied air attack on Germany had met with little success, but by the winter of 1943–4, the Allies had virtually complete control over Europe's skies.

RECOLLECTION

"They were in a small field and the houses on one side were alight. A great flame was shooting straight toward them—a flame as high as the houses and nearly as wide as the whole street. As she stared in fascination, the giant flame jerked back and then shot forward toward them again. 'My god, what is it?' she said. 'It's a firestorm,' the man replied. 'In a minute there'll be dozens like that. We must run.'"

The use of incendiary (fire) bombs could cause "firestorms"—gusts of flame at 1832°F that traveled over 100 miles (161 km) an hour.

E.Wendell describing the Allied bombing raid on Hamburg in *Hausfrau at War,* 1957.

Toward the end of the war, Allied Bomber Command could regularly send more than 1,500 aircraft on a single operation. Most of these were the four-engined *Lancasters* (Britain's best long-range bomber), which had a huge range and could carry bombs of up to ten tons.

Navigational aids had also been greatly improved. At the outset of the war, British bombers had to rely on a map, watch, and compass, and bombs rarely found their targets. Scientists invented navigational aids; a pathfinder force was created to drop flares (which lit up areas to be bombed) and incendiaries (firebombs) to help the bombers find their targets more easily. Despite the Allied mastery of the air, casualties among the crew were terrifying, with perhaps only 20 percent of them surviving a 30-hour tour of duty, and falling victim to Nazi fighters.

The Unied States' entry into the war brought major resources to the Allied side, including aircraft. The massive 8th Air Force joined the RAF in 1943. Although British Bomber Command had attacked industrial areas, they had also bombed German cities. The U.S. 8th Air Force wished to focus on key industries and this meant bombing in daylight. This was very risky because it meant that they would be at the mercy of German fighters, but the U.S. commanders believed that they would be so heavily armed with machine guns they could survive.

Cities such as this one were destroyed by the Allied aerial bombing of Germany.

Allied aircraft began to fly deep into Germany but had to call a halt to their operations because of German fighter attacks. Their own fighter escorts did not have enough fuel to accompany them all the way to Germany and back. The U.S.'s answer was to start a rapid program to build thousands of long-range *Mustang* fighters as escorts. These could fly from RAF bases as far away as Berlin, and could provide all the protection the bombers needed. The Germans were unable to keep up the same level of aircraft production as the Allies, nor could they replace the crews that had been killed. By 1944, many German pilots had very little flying experience. Aircraft fuel had practically dried up since many oil depots had been destroyed.

The Battle of Berlin

After the failure of the Battle of the Bulge (see page 37), the way was now open for U.S. and British forces to cross the Rhine into the heart of Germany itself. Meanwhile, Stalin ordered his generals to launch an immediate attack on the capital, Berlin. He was anxious to take the city before the British and the U.S. forces arrived, so that he could claim the final victory. It also meant he would control the capital of Germany and might have a hand in its future. He split his forces between Marshal Georgi Zhukov, the most successful commander in the Soviet army, who attacked from the north, and Marshal Ivan Konev, who attacked from the south. This triggered a race between the two commanders, who were both eager to be given the credit for the fall of Berlin.

More than a million shells were fired into the city and its surrounding area. However, when the Soviets sent their infantry into the attack, they were repulsed by German forces who had prepared secure and well-dug-in positions. It took Zhukhov three days to batter his way through the German defenses, and his army suffered huge casualties. The Soviets lost scores of tanks and over 30,000 men in Stalin's desperate haste to take the capital.

Amid the rubble of the city, Hitler held out in his underground bunker, still making plans to repulse the enemy with imaginary forces. The remnants of his armies attempted a counterattack but the slaughter was terrible, with the wounded left by the roadsides. More than 50,000 soldiers died in this last desperate stand. Hitler was now left with only the old men of the Home

SOURCE

RECOLLECTION

"We started to fire at the masses. They weren't human beings for us. It was a wall of attacking beasts who were trying to kill us. You, yourself were no longer human."

A former German machine gunner describing the Soviet attack on Berlin in April 1945.

Guard (a part-time army) and young teenage boys of the Hitler Youth for support, and they stood little chance against the experienced Soviet army.

On April 30, 1945, Hitler finally realized that his ambition to create *"the thousand year Reich"* was at an end. Along with his mistress, Eva Braun, he committed suicide in his underground bunker, leaving instructions for his aides to burn their corpses. On May 4, the German High Command officially surrendered to the Allied forces, and the following day, Admiral Karl Dönitz of the Germany Navy ordered all naval forces to return to base. On May 8, 1945, the war in Europe officially came to an end.

SOURCE

NEWSPAPER

Below is the front cover of *The Call Bulletin* newspaper from May 8, 1945. The headline celebrates Victory in Europe, V-E day.

Japan surrenders

Two months after Germany had surrendered, in July 1945, U.S. scientists successfully carried out their first atomic bomb test. Although the United States was winning the war against Japan, the cost in human casualties was immense. Nearly 7,000 troops had been killed in the fighting to take the island of Iwo Jima in the

SOURCE

RECOLLECTION

"I climbed on top of a pile of corpses. Layer upon layer of them. Some were still moving, still alive. I had to get over them. I can still hear the cracking of their bones."

A survivor remembering the atomic bomb attack on Hiroshima.

Pacific in February 1945, and over 13,000 had died in the battle for an island near Okinawa. It was expected that even more would die once U.S. forces landed on mainland Japan, where there would be stiff resistance.

At a conference of the Allied powers in Potsdam on the outskirts of Berlin in July 1945, the U.S. decided to inform the Japanese government that unless they surrendered, the atomic bomb

would be used against them. Japan refused, fearing that surrender might mean the end for their emperor and their national identity.

On August 6, 1945, a B-29 bomber, *Enola Gay,* flew over the city of Hiroshima carrying a nuclear bomb. It was 8:15 a.m. on a beautiful summer morning. The plane doors were opened and the massive bomb, weighing 10,000 lbs, was released. The tail gunner (machine gunner in the back of the bomber) was momentarily blinded as a ball of fire with a temperature of 180 million °F burst over the city.

Five square miles (8 sq km) of the city were turned to dust. Eighty-thousand people died in that instant, and many thousands more suffered a slow and agonizing death from radiation poisoning in the weeks that followed. One airman aboard the *Enola Gay* exclaimed: *"My God, what have we done?"* Still the Japanese government refused to surrender. Three days later, a second atomic bomb was dropped on another Japanese city, Nagasaki, with similar devastating results. On September 2, 1945, the Japanese officially surrendered.

(opposite page) This photograph was taken from a U.S. observation plane at 11:00 a.m., August 9, 1945. Six miles (10 km) below, Nagasaki is a blazing inferno, 40,000 people are already dead and another 60,000 seriously injured.

The terrible price of World War II

World War II had been fought on a scale never seen before. Fighting occurred in most of the continents of the world and the death toll was immense. Nazi aggression had cost about 38 million lives; the Soviet Union paid the highest price with 20 million dead. Japan's aggression had cost the country 1.2 million lives. These figures do not include the six million Jews who were murdered in the death camps in the Holocaust at the hands of the Nazis. Warfare had changed beyond all recognition. The invention and use of the atomic bomb and the development of new missiles created the fear of the future total annihilation of humankind that persists to this day.

For the time being in 1945, however, the end of the war was greeted with enthusiasm. On V-E (Victory in Europe) day, celebrations and parties were held everywhere, by people who were thankful that the slaughter was, for now, at an end.

Parisians crowd the streets to celebrate the end of war in Europe. This picture was taken on May 16, 1945.

TIMELINE

1933
January — Adolf Hitler appointed as chancellor of Germany.

1937
July — Japan invades China.

1939
September — Germany invades Poland.

1940
April — Germany invades Denmark and Norway.

May — Germany invades Belgium, the Netherlands, Luxembourg, and France.

June — France surrenders to Germany.

July — Battle of Britain begins.

September — Italian forces invade Egypt. Germany postpones plans to invade Britain.

December — British forces push back Italians in North Africa.

1941
February — Rommel arrives in North Africa.

April — Record number of sinkings by German U-boats.

April — German forces invade Greece and Yugoslavia in Balkans *blitzkrieg*.

June — Operation Barbarossa, the attack on the Soviet Union by Germany begins.

December — Britain and the U.S. declare war on Japan.

Germany declares war on the U.S.

1942
January — Invasion of Burma by Japanese. Singapore falls to Japan.

May — Battle of the Coral Sea begins.

June — Battle of Midway.

August — U.S. troops land at Guadalcanal.

August — Battle of Stalingrad begins.

November — Germans beaten back at El Alamein. Operation Torch begins—Allied landings in North Africa.

1943
February — German 6th Army under von Paulus officially surrenders in Stalingrad.

March–July — Air raids on German industry begin.

May — German and Italian troops surrender in North Africa.

July — Battle of Kursk.

1944
January — Allies land in Italy.

February–May — Battle of Monte Cassino.

June — D-Day Landings in France.

September — British forces launch unsuccessful attack at Arnhem in Normandy.

December — Battle of the Bulge.

1945
March — Allies cross the Rhine.

April — Soviets launch attack on Berlin. Hitler commits suicide.

May — Germany surrenders.

August — Atomic bomb dropped on Hiroshima and Nagasaki.

September — Japan formally surrenders.

GLOSSARY

Aircraft carrier
A large ship with a deck from which aircraft can take off and land.

Amphibious assault
An attack from the sea with land forces.

Armor
Heavy metal plating on vehicles to protect them against enemy fire. Armored warfare is the use of metal-plated vehicles such as tanks.

Artillery
Engines that discharge large weapons in war.

Asdic
Radar equipment aboard a ship to detect submarines.

Battle cruiser
Lightly armored warship, faster than a battleship.

Battleship
A large ship armed with heavy guns.

Blanket bombing
Heavy aerial bombing of cities.

Blitzkrieg
"Lightning War"—fast-moving war with armored divisions.

Bunker
An underground shelter built for troops.

Communism
The theory of an economic and social system in which everyone is equal and where all property is owned collectively by the people.

Conscription
Involuntary draft to the armed services.

Convoy
Merchant ships sailing close together, usually with an armed escort, for safety.

Destroyer
A medium-sized ship armed with guns and torpedoes.

Detonate
To explode or make something explode.

Devastator torpedo bomber
The most modern and effective torpedo bomber in WWII.

Dictator
An individual who has total control over a country.

Dive-bomber
An aircraft armed with bombs that are released in a steep descent.

Empire
A geographical area that is owned and controlled by a particular government or country. For example, the British empire controlled many overseas areas in the twentieth century.

Fascism
An extreme political movement based on nationalism, and usually, military authority that aims to unite a country's people into a disciplined force under an all-powerful leader.

Front line
First line of confrontation in a war.

Glider
An aircraft first used by the Germans in WWII. Gliders were towed in the air by military planes. When released, they could glide to landing without the use of an engine. Gliders could carry ten soldiers to a precise target very quietly.

Guerrilla operations
Unconventional combat using surprise tactics.

Holocaust
Deliberate attempt by the Nazis to kill all the Jews in Europe.

Hurricane
A British plane that fought in WWII.

Ideology
An organized collection of ideas.

Lancaster
Britain's main bomber aircraft.

Maginot Line
French fortifications built between the wars along the frontier with Germany.

Messerschmitt
German fighter aircraft.

Morale
A measurement of confidence and hope.

Nationalist
A person who is passionately loyal to his or her own country.

Paratroopers
Troops dropped by parachute.

Propaganda
Information or publicity put out by an organization or government to spread and promote a policy or idea.

Radar
A system for detecting approaching aircraft.

RAF
The British Royal Air Force.

Reconaissance
A survey to find out enemy positions.

Reich
The German Empire.

Ruse
A clever trick or plot used to deceive others.

Shell
A piece of ammunition fired from a gun; it is also called a cartridge.

Soviet Union
Union of Soviet Socialist Republics (U.S.S.R.). A communist state that existed from 1922–1991.

Spitfire
Highly successful British fighter plane.

Stalemate
A situation where neither side gains the upper hand.

Straggled
To wander away from a path or an organized group.

Submarine
A boat built to operate and travel for a long time underwater.

Theaters of war
The key geographical areas of conflict in a war.

Total war
A conflict in which nations mobilize all resources to engage in war.

U-boat
German submarine.

Wolf packs
Groups of German submarines.

FURTHER INFORMATION

FURTHER READING

Band of Brothers by Stephen E Ambrose, Pocket Books, 2002

Barbarossa by Alan Clark, Cassell Military, 2004

Challenge for the Pacific: The Bloody Six-Month Battle of Guadalcanal by Robert Leckie, Da Capo Press, 1999

D-Day June 6, 1944 by Stephen E Ambrose, Pocket Books, 2002

Documenting World War II: The Eastern Front by Simon Adams, Rosen Young Adult, 2008

Documenting World War II: War in the Pacific by Sean Sheehan, Rosen Young Adult, 2008

Stalingrad: The Fateful Siege: 1942-1943 by Antony Beevor, Penguin, 1999

The Atlantic Campaign by Dan Van der Vat, Birlinn Ltd, 2001

Web Sites
Due to the changing nature of Internet links, Rosen Publishing has developed an online list of Web Sites related to the subject of this book. This site is regularly updated. Please use this link to access this list:
http://www.rosenlinks.com/dww/batt

PLACES TO VISIT

The National Museum of the Pacific War, 340 East Main Street, Fredericksburg, Texas 78624

U.S. Air Force Museum, 1100 Spaatz Street, Wright-Patterson Air Force Base, Ohio 45433

U.S.S. Arizona, 1 Arizona Memorial Place, Honolulu, Hawaii 96818
Memorial and museum commemorating the Japanese attack on Pearl Harbor.

INDEX

Numbers in **bold** refer to illustrations.